**SAINT TERESA OF ÁVILA: AN INTRODUCTION**

Mary T. Malone returned home to Ireland in 1997 having taught for almost forty years in St Augustine's Seminary, Toronto, and in the University of St Jerome's, the Catholic College of the University of Waterloo. The author of several books, her latest work on the Women Doctors of the Church will be published by Veritas in the autumn.

# Saint TERESA of ÁVILA

## An Introduction

VERITAS

Published 2015 by Veritas Publications
7–8 Lower Abbey Street, Dublin 1, Ireland
publications@veritas.ie
www.veritas.ie

ISBN 978 1 84730 625 8



10 9 8 7 6 5 4 3 2 1



A catalogue record for this book is available from the British Library.

Designed by Padraig McCormack, Veritas

Printed in Ireland by SPRINT-print Ltd, Dublin

*Veritas books are printed on paper made from the wood pulp of managed forests. For every tree felled, at least one tree is planted, thereby renewing natural resources.*

# Contents

# SAINT TERESA OF ÁVILA: A Blessed Life

Mary T. Malone

# The Road to God

Teresa de Cepeda y Ahumada – Teresa of Ávila as she would become known – was born on 28 March 1515 into a fairly wealthy and aristocratic family in Ávila in Castille, in the centre of Spain. When her father Alonso's first wife died, he married fifteen-year-old Dona Beatriz de Ahumada who bore him ten children, including Teresa, before she passed away at the age of thirty-three. Her mother's death left the teenage Teresa bereft and marked a distinct turning point in her life. She was sent to a convent boarding school, where she showed the first signs of the mysterious illnesses that she was to endure throughout the first forty years of her life. As a result she had to return home to her father's house and, while confined to bed, developed a passion for reading, through which she sought guidance in following her thirst for God.

Against her father's wishes, Teresa later entered the Carmelite convent of the Incarnation in Ávila. This convent followed the mitigated rule of Carmel, the only form then available to either nuns or friars. It was not a happy experience for Teresa, and entailed another spell in her father's house as she struggled to deal with poor health. In 1537, at the age of twenty-two, she had been professed as a member of Carmel. As Teresa was persevering in her efforts at living a spiritual life, it seemed to her that constant prayer and poverty should be the hallmarks of the Carmelite life.

From 1554 on, Teresa's energies were focused on the reform of Carmel. It is this that brought unity and joy to her life, and despite, as she says herself in her letters, the opposition of duplicitous clerics, awkward bankers and much internal Carmelite opposition, she never experienced such severe ill-health again. In 1562, at the age of forty-seven, Teresa founded her first reformed Carmelite house, the monastery of St Joseph in Ávila.

# A Life of Holiness

Throughout the centuries many women mystics prayed *ut unum sim*, 'that I may be one'. It was a prayer for integration of body and spirit, earth and heaven, human and divine. It was a prayer for unity which was the goal of all mystical life and prayer. There is no evidence that Teresa ever used this actual form of the prayer – for one thing, she did not know much Latin – but her whole life was a living out of this prayer for integration. It was a struggle for Teresa that marked her journey from a divided heart to a unified heart. Teresa's whole life was a search for holiness, and since our definitions and experiences of holiness vary from age to age, it is worth asking what exactly holiness was considered to be in the sixteenth century. All Christian ideas of holiness centre on the life and humanity of Jesus. Holiness is living the fullness of humanity in imitation of the life of Jesus. As John of the Cross, Teresa's younger contemporary and close friend, suggested, 'In the eternal silence, God uttered one word, and that was Jesus.' That mcans that when we speak of holiness, we are not speaking of morality but of a kind of co-naturality with God through the imitation of the human life of Jesus. A later saint, Vincent de Paul, said that he never understood the journey towards God until he started praying to Jesus by name. When we speak of mysticism, especially in the case of Teresa, we meet her descriptions of her ecstasies and locutions, especially at the beginning of her journey.

Teresa names these experiences *gustos* and *regalos*, but are, in traditional classical spirituality called consolations and delights. In the highly fevered spiritual atmosphere of sixteenth-century Spain, these experiences were not unusual and deeply admired. In twenty-first-century spirituality, such experiences might warrant intense ecclesiastical and psychological investigation. Nevertheless, as Teresa advanced in the spiritual life, she discovered, as all the saints do, that this union with God and this love of God is two-fold love of God that is lived out in love for others, all others.

# The Historical Context

In Teresa's time the greatest conflict the Church had to face was the complete division of Christianity into various denominations after the Protestant Reformation. Moreover, following the Spanish and Portuguese conquests, came the realisation that there were vast swathes of the world that had never even heard of Christianity. Since several of Teresa's brothers were among the *conquistadores*, she was very much aware of the discovery of the 'new worlds'.

In 1517, Martin Luther nailed his theses to the door of Wittenberg Cathedral, and set in motion the total division of Christianity. Eventually, in response, Pope Paul III summoned the Council of Trent in 1545 and initiated the creation and reform of the Roman Catholic Church. The Council was – amid the cultural and religious wars that were raging all around it – a rather shambolic affair, but eventually the stern spirit of reform gripped the Church, and intensified the hold on Spain; this would prompt the creation of the Inquisition which was to haunt Teresa during her later life.

All of her life Teresa bewailed the lack of worthy spiritual guides among the clergy and reported several instances of bad direction in her own life. During one of her bouts of illness, she had come upon a book called *The Third Spiritual Alphabet* by Francisco de Osuna. This was a turning point in her life and eventually, at the age of thirty-nine, she experienced a total religious conversion. From Osuna, she learned the art of recollection, or passive prayer, as it was sometimes called. It was this form of prayer that became the bedrock of her spiritual life.

It is difficult to imagine now that various forms of prayer could come under the stern and watchful eye of the Inquisition. This was particularly the case with regard to women, for whom any form of advanced prayer was seen to be a very rare gift and needed to be carefully supervised. Women were not generally considered then to be capable of an inner life, and vocal prayer and the practice of virtue were the forms of spirituality recommended to them.

## A Scribe for Christ

In 1562 Teresa wrote her first book, *The Book of My Life*, and became something of a household name among all those in Europe who were searching for guidance in their spiritual lives. Indeed, it was this book, as well as Teresa's other writings, which was partly responsible for spreading what was later called the Tridentine Reform all over Europe. The Council of Trent itself did not close until 1563 and was mostly concerned with the outer institutional life of the Roman Catholic Church. But it was the work of Teresa and of the new Jesuit priests and other new religious orders that attended to the inner life of believers.

Teresa realised early on that her new convents created new needs, and so, in fairly quick succession, she provided guidance for them. *The Way of Perfection* appeared in 1565 and this was followed in 1573 by *The Book of the Foundations*. In these writings, Teresa lays out her intentions for the Reform in quite specific detail, emphasising the need for constant prayer, seclusion and poverty.

By the time Teresa died on 4 October 1582, she had founded sixteen more reformed Carmels all over Spain for the nuns, and together with John of the Cross, over a dozen monasteries for the friars. From the last decade of her life we also have over four hundred letters, which wonderfully illustrate her practical wisdom, her humanity and also her real frustrations as she is opposed and vilified on all sides. As she tries to lead her nuns along the path of reform, she occasionally gives in to outbursts of humorous frustration. In a letter to a nun in 1576 she writes: 'God preserve my daughters from priding themselves on their Latin.' This was partly because Teresa always took the side of the ordinary people against what she called the 'learned men'. This is a remarkable trait of so many women saints and mystics. As the 'learned men' emphasise the rarity of God's gifts, the women welcome all – women and men – to enter the way of perfection, and provide the ingredients for following this life.

## The Interior Castle

Teresa's greatest attempt at speaking about the journey into God's presence is *The Interior Castle* which was written in a few months during one of the most testing and frustrating times in Teresa's life, where attempts were being made by ecclesiastical authorities to dismantle all her work of reform. It was started in mid 1577 in Toledo and finished by the end of the year in Ávila. *The Book of My Life* was still in the hands of the Inquisition, and her spiritual director asked her to write another book on prayer, now in her more mature years. She was instructed to write it in the third person, so that it would not be taken as her own personal testimony. The soul here is seen as a beautiful castle with multiple dwellings at each of seven stages. The first three stages illustrate the process of becoming a good and mature Catholic believer. Much human effort is involved and the whole journey depends on cooperation with the grace of God, calling from the inner sanctum of the soul. The last four stages are what Teresa called 'passive prayer', which is close to what we might today call 'centring prayer'. God dwells in the centre of this castle and the human body provides the outer layer. Notice here that by using such images, Teresa bypasses much of the dualism of soul and body which was traditional in Christianity and commonplace in her time.

## The Spanish Inquisition

Pope Sixtus IV established the Spanish Inquisition at the request of the Spanish monarchs. It inaugurated the expulsion of the Jews from Spain in 1492, and the attempt to make Spain into a totally Christian country with only those of pure Spanish blood allowed to live within its borders. The Inquisition, represented by three inquisitors in every diocese, examined people's ancestry, pored over the rules and constitutions of religious orders, and closely inspected all writings for breaches of orthodoxy. In 1559, the *Index of Forbidden Books* was published, and included on the list was Teresa's old guide, Francisco de Osuna and many others. Teresa's bookshelves and all convent bookshelves had to be emptied of the offending books. Teresa's *Book of My Life* was also picked up by the Inquisitors and it was in order to provide an alternative, and in fact much more detailed and profound book on prayer, that Teresa wrote her classic, *The Interior Castle*, in 1571, in a mere five months.

## Teresa's Teachings

Teresa died on 4 October 1582, but that was the day when the new Gregorian calendar replaced the old Julian one. As a result, eleven days were lost from that month, and so the feast of Teresa is celebrated on 15 October. Teresa was beatified in 1614, and canonised in 1622 on the same day as Ignatius Loyola, the founder of the Jesuits; Francis Xavier, the great missionary to the East; and Philip Neri. In 1617, Teresa had been named as Patron of Spain and on 27 September 1970, she and Catherine of Siena were named as the first women Doctors of the Church. It is therefore to the teaching of Teresa that we now turn our attention.

The world of Teresa of Ávila is totally bound up in her native Spain, then one of the most powerful nations of the world. Teresa rarely mentions the pope or ecclesiastical affairs outside of Spain, but she knew Spain intimately, having travelled from end to end founding her reform monasteries. When Pope John Paul II visited Ávila in 1982 on the 400th anniversary of her death, he called her

'God's vagabond'. Teresa travelled from Salamanca and Valladolid to Granada and Burgos, the last monastery she founded, and many points in between. She had to deal with bishops and nuncios, Carmelite superiors who were in turn either supportive or hostile, not to mention bankers and builders, town and city officials, as well as dealing with the multiple internal problems of a new community and also the one she was abandoning. In the midst of all this, she was writing hundreds of letters and her extraordinary books. She was what one might call a 'practising mystic', if that is not a contradiction in terms. At around the age of forty-six, she tells us that she received divine permission to disobey her superiors. This seems to have applied more to her inner life than to her external activity, which was always complex and exhausting. At a time when fully one-quarter of Spain's population was devoted to the Church, Teresa stands out as a woman of intense self-awareness and self-confidence. Indeed one could say that her writings, in particular *The Interior Castle*, are a course in self-awareness. Many of her male commentators describe Teresa as 'having all the complexity of a feminine mind', whatever that means, but it fails to do justice to this intriguing woman.

Like so many other mystics, Teresa learned her humanity from the humanity of Jesus. Indeed, Teresa's life would have been so much easier if there had been a continuous account of women's mysticism, as she repeats much of what had been expressed before by Mechtilde of Magdeburg and Marguerite Porete, to name but two. Since women were not allowed to teach, as Teresa knew well, and was so often reminded, there was no effort made to paint the ongoing development of the particular strains of mysticism that were so essential to women. So, in a sense, Teresa and every woman had to start from scratch. One element of scripture appears in the mysticism of these women, and that is Proverbs: 'I was daily God's delight, rejoicing before him always, rejoicing in his inhabited world and delighting in the human race.'

## Teresa as Mystic

In the most general sense, mysticism is the experience of direct access to God. It is an experience, not an intellectual discussion. This sense of direct access to God has always been problematic in a Church, which is centred on the notion of the clerical mediation of God's grace and presence. Mystics can, and often do, give the impression that they have no need of the clergy. John of the Cross, himself a Carmelite, did not need to fear this, but women mystics were shrouded in cautions and, in Teresa's time, inquisitorial anxiety. Most male mystics, including many of Teresa's early directors, saw mysticism as a rare and rarely bestowed gift, reserved only for the few. On the contrary, most women mystics saw mysticism as the natural inheritance of every baptised Christian. All were invited to walk this path, and the overwhelming response to Teresa's writings shows how the world was waiting for just such an invitation.

Teresa's main aim in her reform was to provide space for the experience of the presence of God, so that the whole of life could be a constant prayer, in a process of divinisation. It was a process of decentring the self and making a space for love, a process of emptying the heart of all extraneous desires, and especially, as she saw in Spain, a process of moving away from the search for honour. Much of sixteenth-century spiritual theory had emphasised the increasingly abstract nature of mystical prayer, to the extent that as one grew, one moved away from the humanity of Jesus to concentrate only on transcendence. Teresa discovered the falsity of this and instead made the humanity of Jesus the centre of her prayer. Moving away from the human Jesus, she said would be 'an act of high treason'.

Many commentators on Teresa's prayer life divide it neatly into twelve years of the prayer of quiet, eleven years of the prayer of union, and ten years of the prayer arising out of spiritual marriage. Life, and especially the 'seasons of the soul' in her words, is more complex than this. Certainly there are stages, but there are always the sheer facts of human existence, and in a life as eternally busy as hers was, such neatness is unwarranted. The true beginning of her life of prayer was the discovery of the prayer of recollection in the work of Osuna, mentioned above. This is where 'the soul collects all its faculties together to be with God'. Teresa, in her endless use of images, says it is a bit like a hedgehog drawing in upon itself. This was the whole purpose of the reform, to provide time and space for this activity of recollection, and, as always with Teresa, she suggests that human activity, though necessary at the beginning, becomes increasingly unnecessary. Without possibly knowing it, Teresa often repeated the thought of the pagan Roman Senator, Symmachus, in his many disputes with Ambrose of Milan, *uno itinere non potest perveniri ad tam grande secretum*, which can be roughly translated as saying that there has to be more than one way to approach so great a mystery. Teresa's gift was to point out these ways, particularly in her masterpiece *The Interior Castle*, but her whole work is laced with images, as she tries to express the inexpressible. It is these images that speak more immediately to us and, like all images, tend to move the heart as well as the mind. She speaks of the soul as a sponge, drawing to itself all the surrounding moisture until it is saturated with the grace of God. She speaks of Jesus as her 'living book' as she has to part with so many of her beloved books after the *Index of Forbidden Books* was published in 1559. The experience of friendship provides her with many images of prayer as intimate conversation, and here, again without possibly knowing it, she is repeating the words of Catherine of Siena. As a friend, we must 'take time to be alone with the one who loves us'. Jesus, the friend, 'never takes his eyes off you'. Teresa, like so many of the other women mystics we know about, had a marvellous capacity for friendship and for conversation. It is somewhat unfortunate that much of the artwork surrounding Teresa of Ávila shows her in a perpetual swoon before God. While such experiences may have happened, we know that Teresa spent most of her life as 'God's vagabond', travelling all over Spain, and almost feverishly founding her monasteries.

## Teresa and Water

One of the best-known images used by Teresa is that of water, especially the comparison of the spiritual life as four different ways of watering the soul, or the 'four waters' as it is called. These superficially simple images contain more wisdom than volumes of mystical analysis, and continue to haunt the mind. The soul of the beginner, says Teresa, is like an arid patch of waste ground, full of weeds and debris, and needs to be cleared and made ready for planting. It is interesting that she does not start moralising here or entering into self-blame, but simply states the fact. So in order to make the ground ready for planting much human effort is entailed, including drawing many buckets of water from the well by hand. This is tiring work, but the results soon become apparent. The water source is outside and must be reached and used with some effort. This is the time for vocal prayer and also observation of holy people, so that we can learn from and be inspired by them.

The second water comes to us by aqueduct, a marvellous result of human ingenuity. Here the water flows much more freely and is more easily accessible. The soul, now watered frequently and with less effort, begins to show all the signs of new growth. This is the time for reading books on the spiritual life and for availing of good direction. The flowing waters of God's presence now nourish the soul and lead it to desire deeper presence and further self-knowledge.

The third water is the stream. Here the water is always available and we are rooted and planted in its ever-present flow. We can now be confident of God's continual presence with us, and so a new sense of calmness enters our life of prayer, and a new sense of restfulness in God. We begin to enjoy the delights of God's presence, what she calls *gustos* and *regalos*, and whole new horizons of possibility open up to us. We enter a stage of 'heavenly madness' as we learn to root ourselves more deeply in the love of God. Also here, the flowers begin to appear, fed from the flowing stream. These are the flowers of good works and love of others.

Finally, the fourth form of water is described in two different ways, either as a heavy shower of rain, or as a spring bubbling up from within. This is the stage of union, where we can say to God, 'No longer I but you'. At each stage, the water needs less effort from us, and the flow of the water gets more continual and refreshing. We experience the abyss of nothingness at this stage, where the reality of God's being and our being is made real for us, and all the blessings of the abyss become possible. It is interesting that for women, this abyss of nothingness is always seen as a gift of blessedness, while for many male mystics, the abyss or desert is seen as a place of loss and torment, and even, perhaps, 'dark night'. Some psychologists link this fruitful sense of the abyss with a woman's womb, and the longing to fill the emptiness within. Whatever the case, this sense of emptiness, of nothingness, shows up in most women mystics. Again, Teresa had to invent her own language and images, because the rich treasury of medieval women's mysticism was not available to her.

The final image with which we conclude this short introduction to the life of Teresa of Ávila is that of the silkworm. For Teresa, the silk worm evoked resurrection – death leading to new life. The worm dies and a beautiful small white butterfly appears. This new life can be insubstantial and must be nourished, but for Teresa it represented another attempt to put theological language on the sustaining experience of divine presence, in all and with all.

# QUOTES AND PRAYERS

# UNITY

May today there be peace within.
May you trust God that you are exactly where you are meant to be.
May you not forget the infinite possibilities that are born of faith.
May you use those gifts that you have received, and pass on the love that has been given to you.
May you be content knowing that you are a child of God.
Let this presence settle into your bones, and allow your soul the freedom to sing, dance, praise and love.
It is there for each and every one of you.[1]

1. This prayer has been attributed both to St Teresa of Ávila and to St Thérèse of Lisieux. See www.xavier.edu/jesuitresource/online-resources/Morning-and-New-Beginnings-Prayers.cfm

Union is as if in a room there were two large windows through which the light streamed in. It enters in different places but it all becomes one.[2]

2. Teresa of Ávila, *Interior Castle*, New York: Dover Publications, 2007, p. 153.

# Search for Holiness

Let nothing disturb you;
Let nothing frighten you.
All things are passing.
God alone remains.
Patience obtains all things.
Nothing is wanting to him who possesses God.
God alone suffices.[3]

The closer one approaches to God, the simpler one becomes.[4]

God save us from gloomy saints.[5]

---

3. When she died, the sisters found a bookmark in her breviary. These words were written on the bookmark in her own handwriting. See www.fatherpius.littleway.ca/pond58.html
4. See www.quoteswave.com/text-quotes/421901
5. See www.faithunited.ca/140914-human-nature-delight

This Beloved of ours is merciful and good. Besides, he so deeply longs for our love that he keeps calling us to come closer. This voice of his is so sweet that the poor soul falls apart in the face of her own inability to instantly do whatever he asks of her. And so you can see, hearing him hurts much more than not being able to hear him … For now, his voice reaches us through words spoken by good people, through listening to spiritual talks, and reading sacred literature. God calls to us in countless little ways all the time. Through illnesses and suffering and through sorrow he calls to us. Through a truth glimpsed fleetingly in a state of prayer he calls to us. No matter how half-hearted such insights may be, God rejoices whenever we learn what he is trying to teach us.[6]

6. Teresa of Ávila, *Interior Castle,* New York: Riverhead Books, 2003, p. 1.

The devil frequently fills our thoughts with great schemes, so that instead of putting our hands to what work we can do to serve our Lord, we may rest satisfied with wishing to perform impossibilities.[7]

God withholds Himself from no one who perseveres.[8]

… it is very presumptuous in me to wish to choose my path, because I cannot tell which path is best for me. I must leave it to the Lord, Who knows me, to lead me by the path which is best for me, so that in all things His will may be done.[9]

7. Teresa of Ávila, *Interior Castle*, London: Thomas Baker, 1921, p. 296.
8. Teresa of Ávila, *The Life of Saint Teresa of Ávila by Herself*, www.digireads.com, p. 66.
9. Teresa of Ávila, *Interior Castle*, New York: Dover Publications, 2007, p. 137.

I used unexpectedly to experience a consciousness of the presence of God, of such a kind that I could not possibly doubt that He was within me or that I was wholly engulfed in Him. This was in no sense a vision: I believe it is called mystical theology. The soul is suspended in such a way that it seems to be completely outside itself. The will loves; the memory, I think, is almost lost; while the understanding, I believe, though it is not lost, does not reason – I mean that it does not work, but is amazed at the extent of all it can understand; for God wills it to realise that it understands nothing of what His Majesty represents to it.[10]

Any true ecstasy is a sign you are going in the right direction … don't let any prude tell you otherwise.[11]

10. Teresa of Ávila, *Interior Castle*, New York: Doubleday, 1961, p. 83.
11. See Roger Housden, *For Lovers of God Everywhere*, Carlsbad, CA: Hay House, 2009, p. 6.

True perfection consists in the love of God and our neighbour, and the better we keep both these commandments, the more perfect we shall be.[12]

The truly humble person will have a genuine desire to be thought little of, and persecuted, and condemned unjustly, even in serious matters. For, if she desires to imitate the Lord, how can she do so better than in this? And no bodily strength is necessary here, nor the aid of anyone save God.[13]

12. Teresa of Ávila, *Interior Castle*, New York: Dover Publications, 2007, p. 26.
13. Teresa of Ávila, *The Way of Perfection*, New York: Dover Publications, 2011, p. 15.

... we shall advance more by contemplating the Divinity than by keeping our eyes fixed on ourselves, poor creatures of earth that we are.[14]

14. Teresa of Ávila, *The Interior Castle*, Santa Cruz, CA: Evinity Publishing Inc., 2009, pp. 51–2.

# Sharing the Love of God

Christ has no body but yours,
No hands, no feet on earth but yours,
Yours are the eyes with which he looks
Compassion on this world,
Yours are the feet with which he walks to do
good,
Yours are the hands, with which he blesses all the
world.
Yours are the hands, yours are the feet,
Yours are the eyes, you are his body.
Christ has no body now but yours,
No hands, no feet on earth but yours,
Yours are the eyes with which he looks
compassion on this world.
Christ has no body now on earth but yours.[15]

15. This poem is attributed to St Teresa of Ávila and is said to be from a letter by the saint to one of her nuns. However, this is disputed. See http://mimuspolyglottos.blogspot.com/2011/11/whose-hands-another-possible-case-of.html

# Recollection and Prayer

The important thing is not to think much but to love much; and so do that which best stirs you to love.[16]

For prayer is nothing else than being on terms of friendship with God.[17]

Accustom yourself continually to make many acts of love, for they enkindle and melt the soul.[18]

---

16. Teresa of Ávila, *Interior Castle*, Radford VA: Wilder Publications, 2008, p. 44.
17. See https://twitter.com/catholicbishops/status/522394135719071744
18. Igor Kononenko, *Teachers of Wisdom*, Pittsburgh, PA: Dorrance Publishing, 2010, p. 114.

It is of great importance, when we begin to practise prayer, not to let ourselves be frightened by our own thoughts.[19]

He has borne with thousands of foul and abominable sins which you have committed against Him, yet even they have not been enough to make Him cease looking upon you. Is it such a great matter, then, for you to avert the eyes of your soul from the outward things and sometimes to look at Him?[20]

Prayer and comfortable living are incompatible.[21]

---

19. Teresa of Ávila, *The Life of Saint Teresa of Ávila by Herself*, Penguin Classics, 1988, v: 13.7.
20. Teresa of Ávila, *The Way of Perfection*, Kingston Upon Thames: Limovia.net, Chp. 26.
21. Ibid., 4:2.

Mental prayer is, as I see it, simply a friendly intercourse and frequent solitary conversation with Him who, as we know, loves us.[22]

You must know that whether or not you are practising mental prayer has nothing to do with keeping your lips closed. If, while I am speaking with God, I am fully conscious of doing so, and if this is more real to me than the words I am uttering, then I am combining mental and vocal prayer. I am amazed when people tell me that you are speaking with God by reciting the Paternoster even while you are thinking of worldly things. When you speak with a Lord so great, you should think of Who it is you are addressing and what you yourself are, if only that you may speak to Him with proper respect. How can you address a

22. Teresa of Ávila, *The Life of Saint Teresa of Ávila by Herself*, Penguin: 1957, p. 63.

king with the reverence he deserves unless you are clearly conscious of his position and yours?[23]

… you must not build upon foundations of prayer and contemplation alone, for, unless you strive after the virtues and practise them, you will never grow to be more than dwarfs.[24]

Souls without prayer are like people whose bodies or limbs are paralysed: they possess feet and hands but they cannot control them.[25]

---

23. Teresa of Ávila, *The Way of Perfection*, New York: Dover Publications, 2011, Chp. 22.
24. Teresa of Ávila, *Interior Castle*, New York: Dover Publications, 2007, p. 164.
25. Ibid., p. 17.

Give me, if You will, prayer;
Or let me know dryness,
And abundance of devotion,
Or if not, then barrenness.
In you alone, Sovereign Majesty,
I find my peace,
What do You want of me?[26]

26. Teresa of Ávila, This is verse seven from the poem 'In the Hands of God'. See printsofgrace.blogspot.ie/2014/03/St-Teresa-of-Avila-poem-In-the-Hands-of-God.html

# Self-Knowledge and Humility

It is a great advantage for us to be able to consult someone who knows us, so that we may learn to know ourselves.[27]

I cannot understand how humility exists, or can exist, without love, or love without humility.[28]

It is no small pity, and should cause us no little shamc, that, through our own fault, we do not understand ourselves, or know who we are.[29]

27. Teresa of Ávila, *Interior Castle*, New York: Dover Publications, 2007, Mansion.
28. Teresa of Ávila, *The Way of Perfection*, Google eBook, Chp. 16.
29. Teresa of Ávila, *Interior Castle*, New York: Dover Publications, 2007, p. 17.

Since God has given it such great dignity, permitting it to wander at will through the rooms of the castle, from the lowest to the highest, let it not force itself to remain for very long in the same mansion, even the one of self-knowledge.[30]

May the Lord lay his hand on all that I do so that it may be in accordance with His holy will; this is always my desire, although my actions may be as imperfect as I myself am.[31]

30. Teresa of Ávila, *Interior Castle*, Lulu.com p. 18.
31. Teresa of Ávila, *The Way of Perfection*, New York: Dover Publications, 2012, p. 34.

# Human Friendships

If this is how you treat your friends, no wonder you have so many enemies.[32]

Their heart does not allow them to practise duplicity: if they see their friend straying from the road, or committing any faults, they will speak to her about it; they cannot allow themselves to do anything else.[33]

32. Mary R. Reichardt, *Exploring Catholic Literature*, Maryland, USA: Sheed & Ward, 2003, p. 91.
33. Teresa of Ávila, *The Way of Perfection*, New York: Dover Publications, 2012, p. 75.

# Love of the Neighbour

It is love alone that gives worth to all things.[34]

Be gentle to all and stern with yourself.[35]

Never compare one person with another: comparisons are odious.[36]

Always think of yourself as everyone's servant; look for Christ Our Lord in everyone and you will then have respect and reverence for them all.[37]

---

34. Jim Forest, *The Road to Emmaus: Pilgrimage as a Way of Life*, Maryknoll NY: Orbis Books, 2007, p. 61.
35. E. Allison Peers ed., *Complete Works St. Teresa of Ávila*, London: Sheed and Ward, 1963, vol. 3. v. 259.
36. Ibid.
37. Ibid., p. 257.

Be sure that, in proportion as you advance in fraternal charity, you are increasing your love of God.[38]

38. Teresa of Ávila, *Interior Castle*, Whitefish MT: Kessinger Publications, 2003, p. 109.

## Courage

To have courage for whatever comes in life – everything lies in that.[39]

## Gender

About the injunction of the Apostle Paul that women should keep silent in church? Don't go by one text only.[40]

## Goodness

To reach something good it is very useful to have gone astray, and thus acquire experience.[41]

39. See Eknath Easwaran, *The Little Lamp*, California, Blue Mountain Publishing, 1981, p. 80.
40. See http://www.art-quotes.com/auth¬_search.php?authid=6724
41. See ocarm.org/en/content/ocarm/Teresa-avila-quotes

## Humility

Humility is truth.[42]

## Journey

The feeling remains that God is on the journey too.[43]

## Mystery

Each of us has a soul, but we forget to value it … We don't understand the great secrets hidden inside of us.[44]

42. See catholic.net/index.php?option=dedestaca&id=1280#
43. Orest Bedrij, *Exodus III*, Bloomington IN: Xlibris Corporation, 2013, p. 172.
44. Teresa of Ávila, *The Interior Castle*, New York: Penguin, 2004, 7.1

## Patience

Patience attains all that it strives for.[45]

## Religion

God save us from gloomy saints.[46]

## Possessions

Thank God for the things that I do not own.[47]

## Prayer

There are more tears shed over answered prayers than over unanswered prayers.[48]

45. E. Allison Peers ed., *Complete Works St. Teresa of Ávila*, London: Sheed and Ward, 1963, vol. 3. p. 288.
46. See http://www.art-quotes.com/auth_search.php?authid=6724
47. See http://www.goodreads.com/author/quotes/74226.Teresa_of_vila
48. See Neilsons & D., *Pride and Humility*, Maitland, Florida: Xulon Press, 2008, p. 276.

# Suggested Reading

*The Interior Castle* was published by The Classics of Western Spirituality in 1979. Teresa's other works are also in the same series.

Peter Tyler, *Teresa of Avila: Doctor of the Soul*, 2014, is the most recent biography of Teresa of Ávila.